T0132354

ABC's for All Ages

Animals

Patty Copper

Archway Publishing books may be ordered through booksellers or by contacting:

Archway Publishing
1663 Liberty Drive
Bloomington, IN 47403
www.archwaypublishing.com
1 (888) 242-5904

ISBN: 978-1-4808-6982-0 (sc)
ISBN: 978-1-4808-6983-7 (hc)
ISBN: 978-1-4808-6981-3 (e)

Print information available on the last page.

Archway Publishing rev. date: 10/25/2018

Also by Patty Copper

ABC's for All Ages:
Musical Instruments
Take Part in Art

To Grant and Adeline
Grrrrrrrrrrr

Come join with me in an exciting
quest to learn about animals
that meow, growl and howl.

A is for Armadillo
they have a hard shell

Birds and Butterflies
their colors are swell

Cheetahs and Camels have
a great sense of smell

D is for **D**ucks they swim
in lakes and the sea

Eagles are majestic in the land of the free

F is for Flamingoes they have skinny legs and are pink

G is for Gorillas they can use tools and can think

H is for Hyenas they can grunt, groan and giggle

Iguanas are lizards and their tails can wiggle

J is for Jellyfish
so graceful as
they sway

Koalas sleep a lot
even during the day

L is for **L**emurs they like
to eat, jump and play

Macaws are large parrots who love the spotlight

N is for **N**yalas they like the water hole at twilight

O is for Okapi a rare mammal who likes to feed on trees

Peacocks have vibrant feathers that move in the breeze

Q is for Quokka they like to hop, hop, hop

R is for Raccoon they will eat your crop, crop, crop

S is for Sloth they hang by their claws

T is for Tigers they have big paws

Urial is a sheep that eats shrubs, plants and grains

Vultures circle overhead in different terrains

Wolfs howl to each other to entertain

Xenotarsosaurus is a dinosaur that is extinct I am told

Yaks have thick fur to survive in the cold

Z is for Zebras they are a site to behold

So play with a
puppy or pet a
fluffy kitten,

then out of the blue,
take a trip to the zoo.

Patty Copper was a high school math teacher for twenty-one years. She lives in Irmo South Carolina, and is enjoying retirement with her husband Mike. Patty has a son and two grandchildren.

Printed in the United States
By Bookmasters